Holding yourself with hope: every situation in life is temporary

Brian c.watson

Table of content

Chapter 1

Surrounding your life with positive people

It's well recognized that practicing a talent alongside with someone who is better than you can help you get better at it, you will need to work harder, think more quickly, and learn more principles. You'll perspire and feel sore, but with practice, your abilities will advance, and someday you might even be able to impart some knowledge to others. It's beneficial to surround yourself with successful individuals since the concept of playing with someone who is more successful than you transfers well to both your personal and professional success.

I recently had the honor of going to the Summit LA18 conference in Los Angeles. I attended keynote addresses delivered over the course of four days by some of the world's best thinkers, businesspeople, and entertainers, including Guy Laliberté, Bob

Weir, Jose Andres, Michael Ovitz, Eckhart Tolle, Gary Vaynerchuck, Tarana Burke, and so many others. I couldn't help but be motivated by all of these remarkable individuals.

When the conference/festival was over, I felt energized and brimming with fresh concepts. I was playing with winners, and talking to and learning from these bright brains inspired me to improve.

Here are some doable actions to help you put this idea into practice in your own life.

Leave The "Negative Nellies" Alone

Everyone has those coworkers who are perpetually troubled or engage in severe drama and who are unable to advance in their careers. Even worse, they can't help but attempt to drag you down with them.

Life is difficult enough; we don't always succeed, and there will always be roadblocks and doubters in our way. Nothing makes you feel better at those moments than having friends or mentors who will listen to you while also encouraging you to be the best version of yourself. "Enter again and perform better! You are capable of doing it. They provide you with energy and aid in your onward motion.

Find and concentrate on connections with people who can inspire you by sharing their successes and good feelings and showing you that you are capable of doing the same. Life is too short to spend it being negative.

Look for People Who Are Smarter Than You.

Many entrepreneurs and business people aspire to be the smartest person in the room on every topic. However, you're essentially restricting yourself if you're constantly the brightest person around. We often undervalue the value of the company we maintain, as Jim Rohn famously observed, "You're the average of the five people you spend most of your time with." We need those who will push us to improve, whether they be instructors, mentors, family members, or close friends.

Setting higher standards for oneself is made possible by the correct circle of influence. We frequently don't realize our potential until we witness what others accomplish.

The popularity and success of organizations like Summit Series, EO, and YPO among high achievers is no coincidence. Positive, successful individuals actively (and unconsciously) push us to be our best selves when we surround ourselves with them.

Develop Relationships With People Who Have Already Achieved Your Goals in "Real Life".

It's time to reconsider our social media usage and put more emphasis on our connections in "real life." The social media feeds of today may frequently serve as a reminder of our limitations, mistakes, and lack of confidence. A person's internet "highlight reel" doesn't fully convey the amount of labor that goes into it or what happens behind the scenes. Spend attention on success's process rather than just its outcomes.

Generally speaking, highly successful people are open to sharing their insider secrets. They may teach you from their experiences and provide you with "tricks and tips" that will enable you to accomplish your objectives more quickly. Find influential people in your profession and meet with them in person.

Watch the match if you can't play tennis instead.

I met several "real life" people who have already had an influence on my life while participating in Summit's LA18 event, which was both motivating and ambitious, but I am aware that not everyone has the opportunity to attend seminars. Or maybe it's just that you don't know them or have access to them, so you can't be around people who have what you desire.

My go-to solution is straightforward: ingest their stuff and turn them into "friends in your brain." For instance, listen to Gary Vaynerchuck's daily podcast if you want to grow your business. Take him along on your everyday commute to work so you may learn from his wisdom, advice, and skills.

Rich Roll was yet another outstanding speaker at the Summit event. Rich has published many books and has a podcast. He will demonstrate how to play the wellness game for you if you don't believe you can.

I dare you to assess, reevaluate, and weed through your online and offline "friends" to locate the perfect individuals and media material that will truly aid you in becoming your greatest self.

Surround yourself with positive people if you want to improve your life.

We've all heard the adage, "You're the average of the five people you spend the most time with," but how many of us randomly choose those five people?

When it comes to self-improvement, the largest error people make is trying to rely solely on willpower without considering how their environment affects them.

Without decent company, you run the risk of experiencing life's same unavoidable outcomes. Spending time with losers will make you a loser as well. The inverse is also accurate.

You would naturally become all three if you spent a lot of time around individuals who were motivated, ambitious, and active because you wouldn't want to be the one that stood out as being the lazy one.

It's no accident that people use group dynamics in settings like reading clubs, group exercise classes, Toastmasters sessions, and AA meetings to promote behavior change.

One of the key components to your success in life is your social circle.

The following false notions must be abandoned if you want to escape situations that neither improve nor worsen your life.

How to Be Surrounded by Good People

There is a way to surround oneself with positive individuals without coming across as harsh, nasty, or cruel. Rarely will you need to be harsh, but generally speaking, you may progressively surround yourself with nice people by spending less time with some and more time with others.

There is a method for doing it without being crafty and manipulative. As a result of the way you're living, you start to surround yourself with wonderful people. I used to regularly use alcohol, go out to parties, and do drugs, so I hung around with like-minded individuals.

By altering myself, I can change my peer group. The more time I invested in improving myself, the less inclined I felt to indulge in drinking, partying, and drug use.

I refused to do these things when my friends asked me to.

Not because I was snubbing them, but rather because I didn't want those pursuits to interfere with my new existence. We spent time in various settings since certain individuals were cool with it. Relationships with those people, whom I only became close to through partying, inevitably ended.

I changed my lifestyle, and as a result, I was able to surround myself with wonderful people. I saw that, both online and offline, I was drawn to people and pursuits that emphasized self-improvement. Making online connections will be crucial for many of you since it's uncommon to run into a group of people who share your enthusiasm for the changes you're making in your life.

Attending community gatherings, organizations, and groups based on your interests are proactive ways to surround oneself with positive people.

The same may be accomplished online through mastermind groups, social media interactions, and networking with others in your area (I met a bunch of writers just through posting content online). Putting your thoughts and lifestyle on display online may attract new people into your life, both virtually and physically.

You'll really meet like-minded people by just leaving the house, mingling with others, and adopting a fresh attitude.

Everywhere you go, seek out partnerships that will benefit both parties and make an effort to gain allies. Instead of entering into every relationship haphazardly or out of proximity, be more deliberate about the ones you create.

This approach is made simpler if you have a personal code for the kind of person you are and what you want out of life. You are aware of who to let in and who to exclude. This is all about their character and has nothing to do with their rank or status in the world. There are obedient individuals without money and wealthy snakes.

There are those who can support you both financially and emotionally. Treat everyone with respect and decency, from the janitor to the CEO, and you'll attract wonderful people to yourself. not for any inherent merit either, but simply because it's the correct way to live.

So you live your life as a wonderful example to others while forming enduring bonds with good people along the way.

You may surround yourself with pals that encourage you to relax, enjoy life, and stop taking everything so seriously (the ones you grew up with are good for this). With high-powered and driven friends and coworkers, it is possible to build more official business interactions.

Make quick friends with all of your town's retail, service, and culinary workers. For book smarts and knowledgeable individuals who may not have the greatest IQs but possess the necessary street smarts to get by in life, hang out with high-cultured, funny sorts.

Hang out with charming and self-assured individuals if you are a timid and uncomfortable person. Spend time with business people if you want to improve your skills in the field. Find several situations of individuals living the lifestyle you desire, and they will influence you.

Chapter 2

Positive thinking

Focusing on the positive aspects of any circumstance is known as positive thinking or having an upbeat attitude. It may significantly affect both your physical and emotional well-being. It doesn't imply that you downplay difficulties or ignore reality. Simply put, it implies that you approach both the good and the terrible in life with the hope that all will turn out well.

Self-talk is frequently the first step towards positive thinking. Self-talk is a never-ending stream of inner dialogue that occurs.

Positive or negative thoughts may come to mind automatically. Your self-talk has some elements of logic and reason. Other self-talk may result from erroneous assumptions that you make as a result of incomplete knowledge or unrealistic expectations.

A person who thinks positively has a growth mindset, which allows them to identify opportunities in challenges and hold out hope for a successful outcome.

Finding the worst in everything and having pessimistic beliefs about oneself or the world are indications of negative thinking. During times of loss, stress, and loneliness, positive thinkers don't always suppress all of their negative feelings or ideas, but they are confident in their capacity to get through these trying circumstances.

Anyone who examines the significance of positive thinking understands that our lives will be more positive the more our ideas are positive. Some see this as the application of psychological concepts: It is nearly impossible for someone to accept anything into their lives that they believe they don't really deserve; if they ever do, they will find a way to destroy themselves.

The basic principle behind all of these many approaches to positive thinking is that in order to attract more pleasant events into our lives, our thoughts and feelings must be "positive." But there's an issue...
The issue is that, even when we are aware of how important being optimistic is, it frequently isn't enough to keep us there. We may have a depressed mood or a gloomy state of mind. We can succumb to rage and hatred. We could feel resentful toward the people or things that have hurt us in the past, or we might feel guilty or embarrassed about the things we have done. All of these things might make it very challenging for us to try to create higher and better ideas.

We've all heard the well-intentioned advice to "remain optimistic," but the bigger the issue, the more unrealistic and Pollyannaish this advice might seem. When positivity seems to be nothing more than wishful thinking, it can be difficult to find the drive to concentrate on the good.

The underlying barrier to positive thinking is that it is hardwired into our brains to seek out and concentrate on dangers. When we were hunters and gatherers, living each day under the very real possibility of being murdered by someone or something in our immediate surroundings, this survival strategy suited us well.

The advantages of optimistic thinking have been shown to not just reduce concern but also to provide a variety of long-term advantages.

Here are a few advantages of adopting an optimistic outlook on life for one's physical and mental health:

1. It eases depression.
2. Better social connection quality.

3.0 higher standard of living
4. improved stress-reduction techniques.
5. It lessens the likelihood of disappointment.

Seven behaviors that promote optimistic thinking

Positive thinking isn't always a natural trait. By intentionally directing your thoughts and feelings in an upbeat direction and doing routines that strengthen your attitude, you may gradually introduce positive thinking into your life.

According to Casioppo, developing a more optimistic outlook or mentality is a learnable lifelong activity that comes with experience and is especially better when shared with others.

The following methods can help you retrain your mind to think positively:

1. Avoid engaging with unfavorable information. Although using social media platforms might help you connect with people and get support from others, they can also have negative effects on your mental health. Your capacity to think positively as well as your self-esteem are all impacted by upsetting news and social comparison. You may detach from negativity and concentrate on the here and now by taking a break from social media.

2. Every day, visualize the ideal version of yourself. You can raise your mood and sharpen your mind by focusing on your "Best Possible Self" (BPS) for five minutes a day for two weeks. Create an image of your BPS in terms of personal, relational, and professional progress at each session. This exercise inspires you to consider your goals while reassuring you that you can achieve them. Positivity in life benefits from having the capacity to believe in oneself.

3. Engage in constructive self-talk. The phrase "my worst critic is myself" is frequently used; however, you should be aware that the language you use to yourself can influence your attitude. Reframe your communication with the voice in your head in order to influence your ideas, feelings, and actions in a more positive direction. By actively altering the way you talk to yourself, you can start to think more positively. For example, instead of thinking, "It's too difficult and I can't do it," shift to, "I'll give it another go from a new viewpoint."

4. Keep an appreciation diary. Making a list of your blessings can encourage you to focus on the good parts of life rather than your troubles. Gratitude is related to improved physical and mental health, enhanced happiness, and a general sense of contentment. It also has positive effects on relationships with others. Because you become aware of how well things are going, keeping a gratitude notebook might help you think more positively.

5. Engage in mindfulness. Consciously participate in the present and practice mindfulness in order to prevent being sidetracked by unfavorable thoughts. Spend some time praising what is right. You may better understand yourself and where your negativity may be coming from by being aware of your thoughts and feelings. Your ability to respond to events with more sensitivity enables you to adopt a more optimistic and effective perspective.

6. Recognize when you are thinking negatively. You need to be aware of your pessimistic tendencies and take steps to change them if you want to think more optimistically. It may be about your job, your social life, or even about you. Concentrate on one issue to address and actively take a more upbeat approach to it. Be self-aware and consider why you frequently have a gloomy outlook on that aspect of your life. You may become a more optimistic person by acting to bring about good improvements.

7. Be among people who think positively. You are significantly influenced by the individuals you spend a lot of time with; thus, their mentality might have an impact on you. Positive thinkers will encourage you to keep expecting favorable outcomes, particularly when it's hard to see the positive side of things. Negative thinkers may make you doubt that things can get better. You'll be more likely to have a good outlook if you surround yourself with happy individuals.

If you try to put these habits into practice every day, eventually they will come naturally to you.

According to Casioppo, "shifting our thinking is a learnable talent that may have profound implications on our quality of life. Being flexible and open-minded in our thinking is how we maintain this mentality.

With positive thinking, you can deal with difficult circumstances by keeping a positive outlook and hoping for the best. With all of its advantages for your emotional and physical health, it is a habit that enhances your wellness. By experimenting with various methods, you can teach yourself to view things more positively, but you'll need to work hard to maintain it.

Negative emotions should be experienced and acknowledged since they aid in problem-solving. Although everyone's emotional experiences are unique, a positive thinker is aware that unpleasant emotions are common and transient.

How to Adopt a Positive Mentality

So, what can you do to improve your outlook? Learning to recognize negative ideas and replace them with more optimistic ones is one of the most popular tactics. Though it could take some time, ultimately you might discover that it becomes more natural to think positively.

Avoid talking badly to yourself.

Self-talk consists of the things you say to yourself in your head. Consider this to be the inner voice in your head that evaluates your actions and interactions with others.

Your self-esteem may decline if your self-talk is predominantly negative. What then can you do to break these destructive self-talk habits? Start observing when you have these ideas and then make an effort to modify them as one strategy to break the cycle.

Keep exercising.

The ability to think positively cannot be turned on or off. Even if you are naturally optimistic, it might be tricky to think positively when confronted with adverse circumstances. The secret to achieving any objective is to stay committed over the long haul. Even if you catch yourself thinking about bad things, try to discover strategies to reduce this and develop a more positive view.

Message From Verywell: It may take some time to become proficient in positive thinking; it is not something that can be learned overnight. To start thinking more positively, it might be helpful to examine your own thought patterns and discover fresh methods to apply a more optimistic attitude to your life.

Develop your optimism

Positive training is similar to working out a muscle: the more you do it, the stronger it becomes. According to researchers, your explanatory style—or the way you describe things—indicates whether you are an optimist or a pessimist.

Positivity is something you may choose to have. You may make the decision to think of ideas that make you feel better, shed a more positive light on trying circumstances, and generally give your day a happier, more optimistic tone. By making the decision to adopt a positive attitude toward life, you may start to break free from a pessimistic mindset and start to see opportunities and solutions in life rather than anxieties and challenges.

Chapter 3

Be self-confidence

An attitude of self-confidence in your abilities and capabilities. It implies that you feel in charge of your life and that you accept and trust yourself. You have a favorable opinion of yourself and are aware of your skills and weaknesses. You can manage criticism, speak assertively, and set reasonable expectations and goals.

On the other hand, poor self-confidence might make you feel insecure, make you docile or weak, or make it difficult for you to trust other people. You might be sensitive to criticism, feel unwanted, or inferior. Depending on the circumstances, you might not always feel self-assured. For example, you could have high levels of confidence in certain areas, like academics, but low levels of confidence in others, like relationships.

Self-confidence is mostly dependent on your beliefs and is rarely tied to your real ability. Your views about yourself are called perceptions, and they may be incorrect.

For example, growing up in a critical or unsupportive environment, experiencing separation from friends or family for the first time, evaluating oneself too harshly, or being terrified of failure are all situations that can lead to low self-confidence. People who lack confidence frequently make mental mistakes.

Being confident in oneself is fundamental to being human.

An individual who has self-confidence typically views the future favorably, is prepared to take chances to pursue their personal and professional objectives, and generally enjoys themselves.
However, a person who lacks confidence in themselves is less likely to believe they can

accomplish their goals and has a pessimistic outlook on themselves and what they expect to achieve in life. The good news is that you can boost your confidence!

You need to learn to deal with any negative feelings that may develop, practice more self-care, and establish a positive attitude towards yourself and your social interactions if you want to build self-confidence.

Things to Be Aware of

By recognizing your negative ideas and replacing them with positive ones, you may develop a positive mindset.

Recognize your anxieties and insecurities while regularly engaging in acts of appreciation.

Set manageable, attainable objectives for yourself and be willing to face the unknown as you go forward in life.

Setting objectives and taking chances are also skills you should develop since overcoming obstacles may help you feel more confident.

Determine your strengths. Everybody is good at something, so identify your strengths before concentrating on your abilities.

Permit yourself to be proud of these. You can express yourself through dancing, writing, music, or painting. Find a hobby you like, then develop a skill that matches it.

Having a range of interests or pastimes will not only boost your confidence, but it will also improve the likelihood that you will find others who share those interests.

Following your passion not only has a therapeutic impact, but it also makes you feel special and successful, all of which may help you feel more confident.

Gaining confidence and believing in oneself even more is made simpler by the presence of additional good aspects in your life.

Making simple adjustments to your daily routine and environment can have a significant influence on your capacity to gain confidence and maintain a happy outlook.

Keep in mind your prior successes.

One of the best strategies to stop self-defeating thoughts and raise low self-esteem? Take some time to consider your previous achievements.

A great way to boost your confidence is to make a list of your achievements. The list will serve as a reminder that you have already done it and can do it again.

Accepting how wonderful you truly are, believing in yourself, and then incorporating this insight into your attitude and personality may be among the hardest things to achieve in life.

But nobody compares to you. The world needs the special contributions that only you can provide.

After all, each of us is unique due to our unique talents, skills, and abilities.
So speaking with confidence is a key to being confident. Tell yourself you are confident, then act as if you are.

Your words become your ideas, and your actions become those words. Therefore, if you keep telling yourself that you believe in yourself, eventually you will start to believe it.

Have the courage to accept yourself for who you are, not what you think others want you to be, and know that you are truly deserving of the life you want. You are a unique individual.

Establish goals

Your expectations are based on your beliefs.

If you have good values, you will think of yourself as a decent person. Additionally, if you have confidence in your own goodness, nice things will come your way.
You'll be happier, more upbeat, and more focused on the future when you anticipate wonderful things happening to you. You'll try to see the positive in other people and circumstances.

For instance, if your belief is that you will have a highly successful life and your value is that this is a nice world to live in, you would anticipate that everything that occurs to you will be beneficial to you in some manner.

For instance, if your belief is that you will have a highly successful life and your value is that this is a nice world to live in, you would anticipate that everything that occurs to you will be beneficial to you in some manner.

You'll become a happier and more upbeat person who others will want to work with and for, purchase from and sell to, and generally help to be more successful as a result of having a positive mental attitude about other people and them responding favorably toward you.

Increase self-esteem

You naturally start to believe in yourself when you take actions to improve your self-esteem, confidence, and self-belief. To assist you in growing to believe in yourself, use these six components for self-esteem building:

Objectives

Having a purpose and a positive self-image are derived from setting clear, attainable goals. Your self-esteem increases with each action you take to achieve your goals. Make a to-do list that divides your objectives into manageable steps.

Interference with others

Find role models that you admire and respect and whose ideals are compatible with your own. As you advance, compare yourself to see how you stack up and learn how to grow better. It's not always a smart idea to compare yourself to others. However, mentors and role models can encourage us to improve.

RECOGNITION

Your self-esteem is boosted when you receive praise from influential figures in your life, such as your supervisor, mentor, or members of your family. You'll be noticed if you work hard to accomplish your objectives. Your confidence will surge, and you'll feel proud.

REWARDS

Real incentives go hand in hand with acknowledgement. As you work toward and earn a bonus at work, a certification or license, a promotion in position or degree of trust, or other status markers, your self-esteem increases.

Reach your goals with confidence.

Self-assurance allows you to succeed in life. And the greatest method to maximize your success is to set out your goals.

Face your phobias.

Stop waiting to do things like ask someone out on a date or apply for a promotion until you are more self-assured. By confronting your anxieties, you may increase your confidence in these circumstances.

Practice tackling some of your insecurities that are brought on by low self-esteem. Even if you're afraid you'll look stupid or make a mistake, give it a shot. Even a little self-doubt might help you perform better. Tell yourself it's only a test and observe the results.

It just feels wonderful to have self-confidence.

Nevertheless, having self-confidence has a host of extra advantages that may help you in business, at home, and in your personal relationships. Here are some of the advantages of developing your self-assurance:

Better performance: You may focus your energies on your efforts rather than wasting time and energy thinking that you aren't good enough. In the end, having greater confidence will improve your performance.

Believing in oneself may improve your resilience—your capacity to overcome whatever difficulties you encounter in life.

Chapter 4

Be patient with yourself

Everything may change quickly in the moment in which we live. There is no routine for a situation like this, no knowledge to draw upon, and no path to take. If there was ever a time when we should exercise patience, this is it, right? Since this is something we have never done before, we cannot expect to do it correctly the first time.

Sadly, far too many of us act the other way. We condemn ourselves for not doing it well enough, judge ourselves for taking too long to catch up, hold ourselves and others to unattainable standards, and expect not to experience typical human emotions.

The ability we all possess to wait for something without becoming irate or offended is known as patience. But the more we have to wait, the more patience we lose. It seems logical that our patience is being tried in the ever-changing environment we live in today. Questions like "When can we resume normal activity?" and "How will school be next semester?" still need to be answered. Or "When will there be significant progress toward racial equality?"

We all need a bit more patience in today's changing environment, both with ourselves and others around us.

Why is patience so important?

Even under the best of conditions, interruptions to our regular routines cause us to feel anxious and frustrated. Consider the following additional stressors:

1. Arranging new social norms and medical standards
2. Struggling with worry and despair about the future
3. Experiencing fury in reaction to racial injustice and police brutality
4. Experiencing both individual and group grief Taking care of new obligations

It makes sense why we are struggling. It is, to put it mildly, tiring.
In our achievement-driven culture, it makes sense that we all want to feel or be better as soon as possible. There is a widespread belief that if we push ourselves, we will drive ourselves to accomplish our objectives. Simply said, this is false.

When we are impatient with ourselves, we reject facets of who we are, pass harsh judgment on ourselves, and use critical language toward ourselves. Do you ever find yourself thinking things like, "I should be accustomed to this by now," "I can't get anything done," or "I'm so fatigued all the time; there must be something wrong with me"?

This is because we fail to support ourselves and put ourselves down. This impatience prevents change. As a result, we get unmotivated to keep trying and give up before we've even begun.

Tips for exercising patience:

One of the most challenging life skills to develop is the ability to remain patient with ourselves and other people. And now more than ever, we require it. Use the following advice to cultivate patience:

1.Put progress before perfection.

Consider for a minute how you might instruct a young kid in a new subject. Given that this is how children learn and develop, you would probably encourage and support the youngster when they make mistakes. So why would you talk to yourself in a different voice?

If a youngster made mistakes or became impatient along the road, you wouldn't hold it against them. We never outgrow the need for kind, encouraging advice, not even as adults. Instead of criticizing yourself for not doing things correctly or not being far enough along, try concentrating on the progress you make and what you learn.

The same is true for others as well. Give others the benefit of the doubt when they behave irritably, unhelpfully, or unkindly toward you, your partner, a neighbor, a coworker, or a stranger at the store. We frequently assume the worst about individuals, yet we seldom fully understand their backgrounds or current circumstances. In these times, we may certainly assume that everyone is struggling. When we occasionally fall short, we all deserve a little grace.

2. Exercise

It takes discipline to develop patience with oneself, just like everything else. According to research, waiting eventually results in more happiness. Give yourself the chance to earn your reward over time, and fight the impulse to indulge in instant satisfaction. Consider the following, for instance:

- At the post office, let someone go ahead of you in line.
- Without interrupting, pay attention to what others have to say before you answer.
- Watch a movie in two parts: the first half on one night and the second half the following.
- When you sit down for a meal, wait a few minutes before starting to eat.

With practice, you'll learn to be more patient. You could even notice that you feel calmer, can reach decisions more quickly, and are generally happier.

3. Lessen tension.

When you have a lot on your plate and a lot on your mind, patience is harder to come by. You are less able to exert the necessary patience-testing effort when you are overbooked or worried. To fix this, examine the factors in your life that contribute to your stress. Try to solve these issues, and where necessary, seek assistance. Take a look at how you spend your time and consider what you can give up to make more time for the things that matter to you.

Self-care done the old-fashioned way is the only effective way to manage stress. Three times a day, three deep abdominal breaths are proven to reduce blood levels of the stress hormone. Other methods of relaxing include body scans, guided meditation, visualization, and mindfulness exercises. Of course, getting adequate rest, scheduling time for exercise, and eating a good diet all help to lower stress (especially avoiding too many sweets and alcohol.)

4. Cease multitasking.

When we try to juggle too many things at once, we get more impatient. We all have a tendency to start one activity and move on to another before finishing it. This method repeatedly shows itself to be unsuccessful. Even worse, you do not perform any of these things properly, which is really frustrating. You'll feel more at ease and achieve a lot more by concentrating on one item at a time.

Put three tasks you want to accomplish the next day on a Post-It note and list them before you go to bed. Prioritize these duties by doing them first, and fight the impulse to let other things take your attention away from them. Research conducted in corporate settings has shown that this tactic dramatically raises worker productivity.

5. Confidently address yourself

The best exercise you can do to cultivate the patience you already possess is to alter your internal conversation. Cognitive behavioral therapy (CBT) is a method for recognizing critical, unfavorable thoughts and creating a more rational frame of mind. Try to be patient with yourself as you learn to be more patient with others, since changing your internal conversation takes time. (Yes, I am aware of the irony in this.) At Therapy Changes in San Diego, a licensed psychologist may offer you targeted advice during this process.

Patience with ourselves and others requires mindful recognition of our humanity and the fact that none of us are perfect. Patience means embracing yourself with self-acceptance and focusing on progress rather than on perfection. It means giving yourself compassion rather than withholding it. It means speaking to yourself with more kindness and empathy, such as:

"I am aware that this is challenging. I am aware of your difficulties, but I have faith in you. You can overcome this.

www.ingramcontent.com/pod-product-compliance
Lightning Source LLC
LaVergne TN
LVHW020524160826
845677LV00015B/3887
9798352091951